Other Books by the Authors:

107 Ways to Stick to It

7 Moments...That Define Excellent Leaders

Leadership Matters: Daily Insights to Inspire
Extraordinary Results

Orchestrating Attitude:
Getting the Best from Yourself and Others

Power Exchange: Boosting Accountability and
Performance in Today's Workforce

Passionate Performance: Engaging Minds and Hearts
to Conquer the Competition

The Nature of Excellence

Winners Always Quit: Seven Pretty Good Habits
You Can Swap for Really Great Results

Sticking to It
The Art of Adherence

How to Consistently
Execute Your Plans

Lee J. Colan and Julie Davis-Colan

CornerStone
Leadership Institute

Sticking to It

The Art of Adherence

Inquiries regarding permission for use of the material contained in this book should be addressed to:

CornerStone Leadership Institute
P.O. Box 764087
Dallas, TX 75376
888.789.LEAD

Printed in the United States of America
ISBN: 0-9719424-5-5

Credits
Consulting and editing   The Baldwin Group, Dallas, TX
Design, art direction, and production   Back Porch Creative, Plano, TX

ad·her·ence
\ad-'hir-əns\ noun

holding fast or sticking by;
consistent with.

CONTENTS

"The problem with American business is not a lack of good ideas, but a lack of follow-through."

– Mary Kay Ash

Introduction

How can I get my team to achieve more?

How can our organization get better results with fewer resources?

How can we improve productivity and morale at the same time?

How can I follow through better?

These questions are being asked today in conference rooms, meeting rooms, production floors and hallways of virtually every organization in America. However, these questions are merely symptoms of a bigger problem. The fundamental question is, "How can we consistently execute our plans?"

Leadership trends **and techniques** attempt to provide the answer as if there **is a magic** formula or secret strategy. However, the sheer **number** of techniques and programs leaves leaders mys**tified and** confused – "What *is* the answer? Is it our **culture? My** team's skills? Our strategy?"

The promises of the **latest** leadership fads blind us from seeing how simple **the answer** really is – not necessarily easy, but certainly **simple.** *Sticking to It: The Art of Adherence* not only **gives you** the answer to the *why*, it also goes a step **further and** shows you *how*.

Do not let the size **of this book** fool you. It is packed with practical ideas **and simple** steps for you and your team. Because your **time is a** precious and limited resource, *Sticking to It: The Art of Adherence* cuts through the information **clutter.** The concepts presented are based on real-**world** experiences that have helped many people and **organizations** stick to their plans.

Knowing why and **how certain** teams consistently execute their plans **will propel** you ahead of your competition. Whether **you** lead an entire company or a small department, **applying** the actionable steps found in this book **will advance** your team to higher levels of achievement...**guaranteed.**

Read, enjoy and **stick to it!**

ADHERENCE EQUATION

Success does not depend
upon the brilliance of your plan,
but upon the consistency of your actions.

What is Adherence?

*H*ow many times have we been told the formula for maintaining a healthy weight is to eat a balanced diet and exercise regularly? Everybody knows the formula, although sophisticated marketers package it in many creative ways. If we all know what the formula is, why is it so difficult to apply it to our lives? The secret to losing weight is not in knowing the formula, it is in *applying* what we already know.

Every year on January 1st, people make new resolutions. It is a time to start fresh, to implement new plans for various areas of our lives. But we all know what happens…about 70% of all New Year's resolutions last less than one month. Many last less than a week or even a day. We do not have bad intentions, it is just that most of us do not stick to it long enough to create a new habit – a new way of behaving.

The same process happens in organizations every day. Leaders develop brilliant strategies and are initially motivated to implement them. And yet, most leaders do not stick to their strategies long enough to complete them and achieve the desired results.

Most organizations understand how to develop a strategy, but many fail to successfully execute it. To illustrate this, consider that in a typical year, 40 CEOs from the *Fortune 200* are removed from their posts. Why? Of course, some had poor strategies. However, the most common reason CEOs lost their leadership position was because they did not fully execute their strategies.

Lack of strategy execution is not isolated to CEOs. Leaders at all organizational levels experience challenges executing their plans. In fact, the greatest challenge for today's leaders is not the lack of well thought-out strategies, but the lack of disciplined execution of those strategies. The game is won not by creating new strategies, but by sticking to your current strategy – it is called **Adherence.**

So how do you achieve Adherence? Based on the experiences of high-achieving individuals and teams, there are three components of Adherence: Focus, Competence and Passion. The relationship between these three components is best illustrated by a multiplication equation:

Focus x Competence x Passion = Adherence

When you think about Adherence this way, the critical role of each component becomes clear. For example, on a scale from 0 to 10, if one component is missing (Focus = 0, Competence = 4, Passion = 8), there can be no Adherence.

$$0 \times 4 \times 8 = 0$$

There is also an exponential relationship between the three components. In other words, a higher level of Focus, Competence or Passion will result in a dramatic increase in Adherence. As you increase each component, you build momentum toward executing your strategy.

A team builds momentum as it adheres to its plan the same way you build momentum when you achieve small goals that lead to bigger goals. The required effort decreases over time as actions become habits, and the momentum increases, resulting in a self-reinforcing cycle of achievement.

The results of building Adherence can be compared to the results of planting a bamboo seed. When the seed is planted and nurtured, it can take up to two years for a sprout to break through the earth. But once it does, it can grow over 100 feet in two weeks! This accurately describes the journey and benefits of building Adherence.

"We are what we repeatedly do.
Excellence, then, is not an act but a habit."
– Aristotle

Adherence and Strategy

*I*f we look at what sets high-achieving individuals and teams apart from their peers, we discover their actual strategies are much less important than their ability to stick to them. A mediocre strategy with strong Adherence will produce better results than a brilliant strategy with minimal Adherence. We can see this relationship in another equation:

Strategy + (Focus x Competence x Passion) = Achievement Level

Adherence

This equation illustrates that the quality of your strategy has only an additive impact on your achievement level. However, Adherence has an exponential impact on your achievement level. For instance, if you had a great strategy – rated a 9 on a scale of 10 – but your Adherence was marginal (Focus = 2, Competence = 4, Passion = 3), your achievement level would be:

$$9 + (2 \times 4 \times 3) = \mathbf{33}$$

What if your strategy was poor? If your strategy rated a 2 on a scale of 10, but you slightly improved your Adherence (Focus = 3, Competence = 5, Passion = 4), your achievement level would increase dramatically:

$$2 + (3 \times 5 \times 4) = \mathbf{62}$$

Small improvements in the components of Adherence result in an 88% increase in achievement level, and that is with a poor strategy!

A study of *Fortune's* Most Admired Companies offers compelling support to this relationship between strategy and Adherence. This study looked at the issue of execution – how well companies have mastered the art of Adherence. The researchers found that all of the companies studied:

> ➣ See strategy as important;
> ➣ Have detailed implementation plans; and
> ➣ Use strategy to help identify what to stop doing.

Surprisingly, these factors are not **what differ**entiate companies that made the Top Ten Most Admired list **in their** industry. All of the companies seem to talk the "plan**ning and strategy** talk." The characteristics that are unique to the **Top Ten** Most Admired Companies and separate them from their indus**try peers** are:

1. Roles are clearly defined for **executives,** managers and employees.

2. Business needs and visions **are communi**cated deep into the organization.

3. Performance measurement is **continuou**s and aligned with the strategy.

4. Leaders are held accountable – **both personally** and for their teams.

It is certainly nice to be recognized **as one of** America's Most Admired Companies. However, bottom-line **results are** also key indicators of an organization's health. So how **do the Top** Ten Most Admired Companies compare in that respect? **Below** is a comparison of shareholder returns for these same **companies** versus the S&P 500.

	Returns of Top Ten Most Admired	Return for S&P 500	Difference
Year of Study	9.7%	-11.9%	+21.6%
Previous 5 Years	25.5%	10.7%	+14.8%

These are pretty amazing differences! **They are** even more amazing when you consider the simplicity of the **four differ**entiating characteristics. Could it really be that simple?

Yes, it is. The difference between the **Top Ten** Companies and the rest of the pack is that they do the basics **exceptio**nally well. The researchers concluded that for the Top Ten **Companies,** strategy execution is not an exercise – it is the focus of every**thing they** do.

"The focus of everything they do" is just another way of saying they have high Adherence to their strategy. These companies know how to create a strategy; but more importantly, they achieve superior results because they know how to stick to it.

The same holds true for high-achieving individuals. They do not do anything mysterious to achieve their results. They do not follow the newest fad or trend. They execute the basics, day in and day out, whether it is how they exercise, eat, learn, invest or work. The critical difference is their ability to adhere to a plan, any plan – that is what sets them apart.

The ultimate competitive advantage, organizationally or personally, is being the very best at implementing a plan. Your greatest challenge is not creating a new plan. Your greatest challenge is adhering to your current plan. **Spend more time on Adherence and less time creating a new plan.**

If you are trying to achieve and sustain greater results for your team, applying the principles of Adherence is your ticket! So let's take a closer look at Adherence. The following chapters describe the success factors for each component of Adherence: Focus, Competence and Passion.

Adherence Enemies

Many leaders do not know why their teams do not consistently adhere to their plans. A key step on your journey toward better Adherence is to understand the "Adherence Enemies" – the most common reasons people and teams do not stick to it.

The four Adherence Enemies will be highlighted throughout the book. You will notice a common theme among them – they all begin with YOU!

As you read, think about your biggest Adherence Enemies and then identify strategies to fight them. As a result, you will immediately start to create a unique and powerful advantage for you and your team.

FOCUS

"If you don't know where
you are going, you will probably
end up somewhere else."
– Laurence Johnson Peter

Adherence Enemy #1 –
The "Ship is Adrift" Syndrome

As a leader, your team sees you as the captain of the ship. Your team needs you to provide focus, direction and clarity. However, the pressures of day-to-day demands can force you to switch between various strategies or look for quick fixes. Giving in to these pressures can diffuse your team's focus.

A leader's inconsistency leaves team members questioning who is piloting the ship and in which direction it is going. **Inconsistency is, in essence, the anti-focus.** Employees wonder, "Why should I put effort into this when something else will be a priority next week?" Inconsistent focus is one of the quickest ways to undermine your credibility with your team.

So, what is the solution for improved Adherence and higher achievement? As captain of your team, set your course and stick to it.

"The secret to success is constancy of purpose."
– Benjamin Disraeli

Focus x Competence x Passion = **Adherence**

Focus is a key distinguishing characteristic of high-achieving leaders and teams. A crystal clear focus helps team members prioritize and more easily connect their actions to the goals of the team, resulting in a greater sense of purpose. Maintaining focus for your team keeps everyone "marching in the same direction." This component of Adherence is the most challenging one for leaders, because work environments create many distractions that can diffuse your focus. However, leaders have more control over their focus than they might think.

High-achieving leaders hone their focus. They know what is most important to their teams and do not let other priorities get in the way. They know when to say "No" to projects and tasks that might diffuse their focus, because they understand their time and energy are limited resources. They cut through a world of complexity to keep things simple – they know simplicity produces teams that are efficient, fast and focused.

Let's look at each of these three success factors in detail:

1. Find your "One Thing."
2. Know when to say "No."
3. Keep it simple.

Find Your "One Thing"

One of our favorite movies is *City Slickers*. In the movie, a group of friends from the city takes a "vacation" at a dude ranch. Curley, played by Jack Palance, is a hard, crusty old cowboy full of wisdom. He gives some great advice to Mitch, played by Billy Crystal, who is facing some mid-life questions. Here is the scene:

Curley: You all come out here about the same age. Same problems. Spend fifty weeks a year getting knots in your rope – then you think two weeks up here will untie them for you. None of you get it. Do you know what the secret of life is?

Mitch: No, what?

Curley: This. (Holds up his index finger.)

Mitch: Your finger?

Curley: One thing. Just one thing. You stick to that and everything else don't mean [anything].

Mitch: That's great, but what's the one thing?

Curley: That's what you've got to figure out.

Great scene...great advice. Leaders have to figure out the One Thing that defines a meaningful purpose for their teams.

The One Thing should answer the question, "Why are we here?" You may think that finding your focus is not critical; but in fact, it is essential to your success. **The most important thing in business (and life) is to decide what is most important.**

Your team's One Thing might be: producing defect-free products; providing the fastest service available; developing leading-edge products; creating relationships that customers cannot walk away from; or meeting the technology needs of other departments. These are just examples – your One Thing has to be *your* One Thing. And it should guide all of your decisions and actions.

Even after you find your One Thing, sticking to it can be a challenge while you put out fires and explore new opportunities. Do not be tempted to think, like many leaders, that you can keep piling on the initiatives and still maintain your team's focus. You may find yourself in the middle of the "Ship is Adrift" syndrome (Adherence Enemy #1). Instead, consider automating, streamlining or outsourcing areas that are not core to your team's operation.

Defining and maintaining your team's One Thing is not as easy as it may sound. For instance, on a scale of 0 (no focus) to 10 (crystal clear focus), if a team's focus is rated a 9 at the leadership level, it is likely to be rated a 6 or 7 among frontline workers. To execute consistently, **communicate your One Thing to every person on your team.**

A laser-sharp focus does not happen overnight. It takes time and effort to refine, reinforce and communicate your One Thing, but it needs to start now. Blurred focus creates confusion, resulting in diffused employee efforts. Stay focused!

"Things that matter most must never be at the mercy of things that matter least."
– Johann Wolfgang von Goethe

Know When to Say "No"

*H*igh-achieving teams are clear about their One Thing and are passionate about it. This powerful combination creates *leadership courage* and enables leaders to make difficult decisions for their teams. Developing leadership courage helps you more swiftly decide to channel resources away from non-critical areas or replace a team member. **The conviction to make tough decisions is a key differentiator of teams who adhere to their plans.** These decisions are not perceived as sacrifices or compromises for those who are focused and passionate.

One important way to demonstrate your team's focus is to say "No" to activities that do not support your One Thing. Saying "No" helped Walgreens outperform the stock-market average 15-fold between 1975 and 2000. At one point, Walgreens owned over 500 restaurants. They decided their future was in convenience drug stores and that they would be out of the restaurant business in five years. They courageously stuck to their commitment, which required saying "No" many times to ensure a redirection of resources to their new future.

Saying "No" also applies to the day-to-day decisions you make as a leader. For example, if you spend two hours in a meeting that does not help your team achieve its One Thing, you pay an opportunity cost by spending time on tasks that do not support your focus. If you find yourself saying, "That was a waste of time," "Boy, that didn't add any value" or "Why was I attending that meeting?" – these may be signs that you need to say "No."

As a leader, you might use meetings as a way to conduct business. When you call a meeting, think about the salaries of each attendee and the potential time they could be working on your One Thing instead of being in the meeting. You decide how to use your team members' time, so make sure you are getting the best return for their time investment. Of course, meetings can **be both** necessary and useful; **but** they can also diffuse your focus if **you do not** know when to say "No."

When planning your team's activities, **create a** "Stop Doing List" in addition to all of the new work you **must perform** to execute your plan. Identify those activities, tasks, **reports,** meetings and projects that do not directly support your **One Thing.** Interestingly, your "Stop Doing List" often has a bigger impact **on your** team's ability to focus than the list of "To Do's."

Saying "Yes" to one thing always means saying "No" to something else. Your time, energy and money **are precious** resources – if you spend them in one area, they are not **available** to be spent in another area. Communicating this message **deep into** your team enables employees to say "No" to non-value-**added** tasks and stay focused on executing your plan.

*"It's only by **saying "No"** that you can concentrate on **the things** that are really important."*
– Steve Jobs

Keep It Simple

Keeping things simple for your team helps them stay focused on your One Thing. For example, a study of 39 mid-sized companies found that **only one characteristic differentiated the winners from the less successful companies: simplicity.** Winners sold fewer products, had fewer customers, and worked with fewer suppliers than other companies in the same industry that were less profitable. This study found that simple, focused operations were more profitable.

The 80/20 Principle (also known as the Pareto Principle) helps explain the power of simplicity. The 80/20 Principle is pervasive in our world:

- 80% of traffic jams occur on 20% of roads.
- 80% of beer is consumed by 20% of drinkers.
- 80% of classroom participation comes from 20% of students.
- 20% of your clothes will be worn 80% of the time.

The 80/20 Principle is also alive and well in most organizations:

- 80% of profits come from 20% of customers.
- 80% of problems are generated by 20% of employees.
- 80% of sales are generated by 20% of sales people.

If the 80/20 Principle exists in your organization, then the most profitable 20% of your business is 16 times more profitable than the remaining 80%. The same logic applies to your customers, products, regions and employees.

The question is, "How do you decrease complexity?" The answer is to focus on your vital few (the 20%). Do not only rely on your instincts to identify your 20% – use data to determine the truth about your team's performance. Look at your processes, systems, customers, services and people to find the 20% that drive the majority of your productivity, activity, waste, conflict or down time.

For example, you may find that only two types of errors cause 80% of the rework your team performs or that only a few team members produce 80% of your team's output. You may also discover that a small number of the services you provide generates the largest amount of activity for your team or that a particular department causes 80% of the conflict for your team.

Remember that your vital few can drive negative or positive results. Once you have identified your vital few, create ways to leverage the ones that *help* your team achieve its One Thing. On the other hand, involve your team in eliminating, minimizing or automating the ones that *hinder* your team's focus.

Keeping it simple keeps you focused!

"Genius is the ability to reduce the complicated to the simple."
– C.W. Ceram

Applying *Personal* Focus

Swimmer Michael **Phelps** is a great example of
maintaining personal **focus**. His clarity of focus enabled
him to perform in **five Olympic** games over 16 years.
In his fifth Olympics **in 2016,** Phelps won five gold
medals after a short-**lived** retirement just two years
earlier. His comeback **required** laser-sharp focus, which
is even more impressive **in** light of the fact that he was
diagnosed with **attention** deficit hyperactivity disorder
(ADHD) in sixth **grade! Phelps** is the most decorated
Olympian of all-time **with** 28 total medals – including 23
gold medals – in **no small** part due to his personal focus.

COMPETENCE

"If a man does his best,
what else is there?"
– General George S. Patton

Adherence Enemy #2 –
Blind Spots

Because your greatest liability is the one you are *un*aware of, you must first know the enemy before you can conquer it. Regardless of how well we know ourselves, most of us have personal and professional blind spots – characteristics others see about us, but we do not see about ourselves. A blind spot is any situation where our perceptions about ourselves are different than reality.

For example, a team leader may feel his team provides excellent customer service, but other teams have created "work arounds" to avoid dealing with them. Another example is the individual who thinks she is a great listener, but everyone else knows she will not stop talking! The problems that arise from blind spots can be challenging for leaders and those around them and can lead to dysfunctional behavior, much like the emperor who wore no clothes.

The higher a leader is in an organization, the more his/her information is filtered. In other words, **the higher the leader, the more organizational blind spots he/she is susceptible to.** As a result, leaders can mistakenly believe their teams possess the skills and competencies necessary to execute a particular plan, when in fact they do not.

The best way to see your blind spots is to ask for, and *listen* to, feedback about you and your team.

"Beware of no man more than thyself."
– Thomas Fuller

Focus x **Competence** x Passion = **Adherence**

Focus and passion will certainly get your team a long way on the journey toward Adherence, but they are not enough. Competence is the bedrock of Adherence. It describes more than just your team's skills and knowledge. Competence represents anything that improves your team's ability to perform, including processes, systems and structures.

Competence is also the component that drives sustained execution of your strategy. As a leader, you hold the key to many critical processes and systems that will enable your team to consistently perform – goal setting, measurement, feedback, recognition, training and communication.

High-achieving leaders know that developing competence helps their teams stick to it. They employ three success factors:

1. Elevate the average.
2. Get systematic.
3. Balance your view.

Elevate the Average

*E*veryone would agree that a key to having a great team is to have great people on the team. In fact, some leaders think that mediocre people + great strategy = mediocre results. This thinking assumes you need great people to achieve great results. At face value, this equation seems valid and logical. However, as Yogi Berra said, "In theory, there is no difference between theory and practice. In practice, there is."

In reality, our world consists of mostly average performers. You have some superstars and you even have some falling stars, but the majority of workers are middle stars. To achieve excellent results with average performers, you must have consistent execution. Therefore, a more realistic formula is:

Average Performers + Consistent Execution = Excellent Results

Of course, you should always hire the best people possible; but the real challenge for leaders is to elicit *consistent* effort from all employees. Since most employees are average, those leaders who elevate employees' performance will set their teams apart.

One of the most basic, yet effective, ways to elevate your team's competence is to define clear goals. (Remember, the Top Ten Most Admired Companies outperformed their peers by doing the basics.) High-achieving leaders keep their teams accountable for measurable objectives and for hitting milestones along the way. To do this, they work with their team members to write SMART goals:

Specific

> What will be accomplished?

> With whom?

Measurable

> How will we know the goal has been achieved?

> How will we measure it? (Quality, quantity, cost, timeliness?)

Attainable

> Can the goal be accomplished?

> Does the person responsible have control over the outcome?

Relevant

> How does this goal support our team's One Thing?

> What is the relative priority of this goal?

Time-framed

> When does this goal need to be completed?

> When are the checkpoints?

The Measurable and Time-framed aspects of SMART goals tend to be the biggest barriers to sticking to it. Make sure you can fill in the blank, "I will know I have achieved my goal when _____." Once you know what result you are trying to achieve, you can determine if you are measuring quality, quantity, cost or timeliness of your performance. Be specific about when you want to achieve your goal – "next year" is not specific enough. Finally, state your goal positively, personally and in the present tense.

Although writing SMART goals can be tedious, those leaders who take the time to do so end up spending less time dealing with performance problems and more time sticking to their plans.

Here are some examples of ineffective goals and SMART goals:

Ineffective Goal	SMART Goal
I will improve my efficiency.	I log all of my tasks into my calendar and prioritize them based on my team's One Thing. I say "No" to my top three time wasters. I do not leave work until I finish all of my "A" priorities.
I will delegate better.	First thing Monday morning, I identify the key tasks for our team that week and match them with team members' skills. I spend 10 minutes with each team member to ensure they know what is required. I provide the resources team members need to complete the tasks I have delegated to them.
I will build a better culture on my team this year.	I have regular meetings with each team member to better understand what I can do to help them succeed. At least once a month, I identify a team accomplishment worth celebrating.

Writing SMART goals is the starting point for elevating your team's average performance. After you have written SMART goals for yourself and your team, it is time to manage performance against those goals – coaching, providing feedback, taking corrective action, and recognizing good performance. Managing employee performance is frequently viewed as an administrative task or a Human Resources program. However, **high-achieving leaders view performance management as an ongoing strategic tool** to elevate their team's average and build Adherence to their plans.

Elevating the average performer dramatically elevates your team's performance. Each member of your team should know exactly what she/he is working toward, its relative priority, how it will be measured and most importantly, how it helps your team achieve its One Thing.

"The most important thing about goals is having one."
– Geoffrey F. Abert

Get Systematic

*E*ffective systems are another way to elevate the average performance of your team. Systems help ensure consistent and predictable execution of your plan. In other words, they build your team's competence.

Systems go way beyond your technical computer systems and include any defined, methodical, predictable way of doing work and making decisions. Systems create positive habits for your team. They help you efficiently and effectively:

> Make important decisions;

> Prioritize work;

> Develop new products and services;

> Plan new projects;

> Select and develop employees;

> Measure performance;

> Communicate with each other; and

> Resolve conflict.

Good systems do not appear by accident. Ask yourself, "What systems have I implemented to help my team members consistently execute their plans?" A sampling of systems that can help your team stick to it include:

> Team calendar or project plan;

> Regular reviews of performance;

> Defined training plan;

> Scheduled team-update meetings;

> Exception reports that identify only tasks that are off-plan;

- Documented customer complaint-resolution process;

- Selection and interviewing process;

- Monthly performance data posting for your team; and

- Standard way of discussing lessons learned after each project.

Your team's resourcefulness is a key to Adherence. An old professor of Lee's once said, "The key to success is not to know everything, but to be able to plug up your ignorance within 24 hours." We think he was exactly right. As a leader, you cannot be an expert in everything your team does. Implement systems to help you quickly gauge if your team is on track and, if not, to identify the cause so you can take corrective action.

Winston Churchill said, "For the first 25 years of my life, I wanted freedom. For the next 25 years, I wanted order. For the next 25 years, I realized that *order is freedom.*" Developing and implementing the right systems creates the order necessary to free you up to work *on* your business rather than *in* your business.

"Our goals can only be reached through a plan, in which we must fervently believe, and upon which we must vigorously act. There is no other route to success."
– Stephen A. Brennan

Balance Your View

*H*igh-achieving leaders are always scanning their environment. They step back to look at the big picture, and they dive into the details. They look at the past to learn from their experiences while planning for the future. They know that keeping a balanced view increases their competence.

High-achieving leaders understand the value of seeing both the big picture and the details. Too many leaders work from a 10,000-foot perspective without having a detailed knowledge of their people or business. Although a high-level perspective is necessary for leadership success, it should be accompanied by an in-depth understanding of your team.

Before you can effectively adhere to your plans, you must understand the details and needs of your team's operations – your cost, profit and customer satisfaction drivers. Leaders who make a habit of ignoring the little things will eventually find themselves ignoring the big things. Taking the time to really understand your business from both perspectives helps prevent blind spots (Adherence Enemy #2) for you and your team.

Another way to balance your view is to look at both the past and the future. Every team has a variety of performance indicators. Teams should understand the different types of indicators, what they mean and, most importantly, how to balance them.

Consider a measurement continuum. The two ends of the continuum represent the two types of performance indicators. **Lagging indicators** are the results of your team's *past* performance – they enable you to see if your plans worked as well as expected. **Leading indicators** are the drivers of your team's *future* performance – they give you early warning signs of problems.

Financial Measures	Customer* Measures	Process Measures	Employee Measures
• Revenues • Costs • Profits	• Complaint resolution • Customer satisfaction • Customer retention *Internal & external*	• Quality • Cycle time • Productivity • Response time	• Employee satisfaction • Employee development • Employee retention

Lagging Indicators   **Leading Indicators**

Past   Future

Many leaders only look at lagging indicators, typically financial ones. These lagging indicators are important to help you understand how you have performed in the past. However, they must be balanced with leading indicators that tell you how your team will perform in the future – six, nine or twelve months from now. A singular focus on lagging indicators gives you little opportunity for corrective action if your team drifts off course. Effective leaders look at both leading and lagging indicators of performance. This balanced view enables them to know what *did* happen and also anticipate what *will* happen.

So, as the captain of your ship, keep a balanced view of your team's performance to increase your competence and adhere to your plans. Chart your course (high-level plan) and ensure the deck is clean (details). While on your journey, check the wake of your ship (lagging indicators) and keep an eye on the horizon ahead (leading indicators).

"Wisdom is your perspective on life, your sense of balance, your understanding of how the various parts and principles apply and relate to each other."
– Stephen Covey

Applying *Personal* Competence

Erin Brockovich-Ellis is a superb example of someone who developed her personal competence. She was a single mother of three young children, with no money and no formal education; yet she single-handedly put together a case to win the largest toxic tort injury settlement in U.S. history. Erin proved that with strong determination and focus, and not much more, you can achieve great things. She built her knowledge in the legal world against all odds and won a $333 million settlement for her clients. Her determination to improve her skills elevated her to expert status in her field.

PASSION

"Nothing great was ever achieved
without enthusiasm."
– Ralph Waldo Emerson

Adherence Enemy #3 –
Negative Assumptions

Your assumptions or view of the world will consistently predict your actions and the results you achieve. Assumptions in and of themselves are not bad. It is how your assumptions influence your actions that make them your best friend or your worst enemy.

As a leader, your assumptions have a significant and lasting impact on your team. Your assumptions affect your responses to other people and situations. Your responses, in turn, directly influence others' reactions to you – when team members observe your behavior, they begin to create their own assumptions about you. These assumptions drive their responses to you, and a reinforcing cycle develops. This cycle forms the limits, either high or low, of your team's achievement level.

For example, if you assume your team can achieve a challenging goal, you will act as if they can, and they will respond accordingly by achieving that goal. On the other hand, if you hold negative assumptions about your team, you will act consistently with those assumptions. You may hear yourself saying, "We will never get this project done in time" or "If only that other department would do their part, we could be successful." Your resulting actions – the way you assign tasks, relate to others or set performance expectations – will likely elicit negative reactions from others. Their reactions reinforce your negative assumptions, and a negative cycle has started.

High-achieving leaders know their behavior tells the truth about their assumptions. They also know their assumptions have a direct impact on their team's ability to adhere to their plans.

The most important conversation you will ever have is the one you have with yourself.

Focus x Competence x **Passion** = Adherence

The most common characteristic of high-achieving leaders, and high-achieving people in general, is a deep sense of passion for their One Thing. Although focus and competence are critical to Adherence, passion is the glue that helps teams stick to their plans over the long haul.

Having passion for a particular goal – personal or professional – provides the energy and motivation to take the necessary actions to achieve that goal. Researchers who study high achievers now consider passion to be the "missing link." It is the intangible component that explains why some people and teams are able to adhere to their plans.

To improve your team's Adherence, develop the three success factors for building passion:

1. Paint the picture.
2. Give what you want.
3. Value your values.

Paint the Picture

*W*e have discussed creating focus and developing competence. These are the things that capture the minds of your employees. To capture their hearts and ignite their passion, we must meet one of their most basic psychological needs – to contribute to something bigger than a job, to find meaning in life.

Picture this scenario: Three people were crushing rocks side by side on a construction job. When they were asked, "What is your job?" the first person answered, "My job is to do what I am told for eight hours a day so I can get a check." The second person replied, "My job is to crush rocks." The third person said, "My job is to build a cathedral."

Which of these three people do you think would be the happiest, most productive and go the extra mile? No doubt the third person, who understood his job was far greater than just crushing rocks. He understood he was contributing to a purpose greater than his own efforts.

When people work hard for something they believe in, a high degree of passion develops. This passion cultivates a mental toughness that enables employees to see opportunities in situations that might be seen as obstacles by others. Creating a sense of meaning for employees and developing that passion elicits discretionary effort and a willingness to sacrifice for the greater cause.

For example, after the economic fall-out of September 11, 2001, Southwest Airlines' employees voluntarily forfeited $5 million in vacation time and $1 million in pay to help the company stay financially viable. Employees also took over the lawn and facility maintenance at corporate headquarters. These employees had a deep sense they were contributing to something larger than themselves – in this case, the survival of their employer (and to many, their "family"). The sense of meaning Southwest had nurtured helped its employees see this situation as an opportunity to contribute rather than something out of their control.

The foundation for creating a meaningful work environment is to help employees see how they fit into the big picture. People will naturally become more passionate about their work when they clearly understand they are a part of something bigger than themselves. As a leader, you must be able to answer the four questions employees commonly ask (and they are asking these questions – whether you hear them or not):

1. Where are we going? (Strategy)
2. What are we doing to get there? (Plans)
3. How can I contribute? (Roles)
4. What is in it for me? (Rewards)

Once employees see the big picture, the next step is to help them find a greater purpose in every project and task they perform. To help make this connection for employees, be prepared to answer the question – "*Why* do I have to do this?" (HINT: The answer is *not*, "Because I am the boss.")

Here are some additional tips for creating a meaningful work environment:

- Draw a clear connection between employees' work and your team's One Thing.
- Give employees the tools and autonomy to take ownership of their goals.
- Challenge employees to develop new skills and areas of knowledge.

Creating meaningful work for your team might seem like a soft, intangible process; but high-achieving leaders know it yields hard, tangible results.

"The more I want to get something done, the less I call it work."
— Richard Bach

Give What You Want

*C*ontrary to popular belief, most employees do not quit their jobs because of compensation or something "the company" did. Employees typically quit because of how they were treated by their direct supervisor. **People quit people, not companies.** And it often comes down to a simple matter of respect.

We all want to be treated with decency and respect. The best way to get respect is to give it first. There are two ways to build respect: use good manners and appreciate the whole person.

Showing respect for others includes demonstrating good manners in obvious ways – smiling; saying please and thank you; using employees' names when you talk with them; and respecting others' time. This sounds like a list that should be posted on a kindergarten classroom wall; but it is amazing how frequently we forget these common courtesies in the course of a busy day.

Here are some other, less obvious, ways to show respect:

> Keep eye contact;

> Greet people before talking business;

> Apologize when late or interrupting;

> Converse instead of lecture;

> Avoid sarcasm; and

> Maintain emotional control.

These simple behaviors deepen respect and contribute to the complex concept of passion – passion for the work, workplace and workmates.

The second way to nurture respect is to appreciate the whole person. This appreciation is not something you turn on and off. Rather, it is woven into your day. Instead of seeing employees as a means to achieving your team's goals, your interest in them should be deeper.

Charles Plumb was a U.S. Navy pilot in Vietnam. After 75 combat missions, his plane was shot down; he ejected and parachuted into enemy hands. He was captured and spent six years in a Vietnamese prison. He survived the ordeal and now lectures on the lessons learned from that experience.

One day, Plumb and his wife were sitting in a restaurant when a man came up and said, "You're Plumb! You flew jet fighters in Vietnam from the aircraft carrier Kitty Hawk. You were shot down!"

"How in the world did you know that?" asked Plumb.

"I packed your parachute," the man replied. Plumb gasped in surprise and gratitude. The man pumped his hand and said, "I guess it worked!"

Plumb assured him, "It sure did. If that chute hadn't worked, I wouldn't be here today."

Plumb couldn't sleep that night, thinking about the man. He thought of the many hours the sailor had spent on a long wooden table in the bowels of the ship – carefully folding the silks of each chute, holding in his hands someone's fate.

Plumb later said, "I kept wondering what he might have looked like in a Navy uniform – white hat, bib in the back, bell-bottom trousers. I wondered how many times I might have seen him and not even said, 'Good morning, how are you?' because, you see, I was a fighter pilot and he was just a sailor."

So, who is packing **your** parachute?

It is easy to appreciate the top performers who bail you out of tight spots. It is more challenging, but more meaningful, to appreciate everyone on your team regardless of their relative contributions.

Remember, at the end of the day, your success is based more on what your *people* do than what *you* do. We all have someone who provides what we need to make us more productive. Focus on the people, not titles.

The length of any given conversation with an employee is less important than the fact that we know something special about them (family members, outside interests, etc.). Sometimes, in the daily challenges life gives us, we miss what is really important. We may fail to say hello; congratulate someone on something wonderful that has happened to them; give a compliment; or just do something nice for no particular reason.

You build commitment to you and your team by appreciating employees and showing them respect in little ways. These actions will enhance the passion your team will show for your One Thing. Give what you want and you will get what you need.

"Constant kindness can accomplish much. As the sun makes the ice melt, kindness causes misunderstandings, mistrust and hostility to evaporate."
– Albert Schweitzer

Value Your Values

*J*ust as important as what your team does is how your team does it – in other words, your team's values. Values help build a common focus and set of norms. Team values might include collaboration, innovation, zero defects or a customer-first commitment.

The word "communication" comes from the Latin root meaning "community." Your efforts to communicate team values play a key role in creating a unique community of employees.

Depending on how you communicate your values, you can build cynicism or passion with your team. Some leaders "sell" their values to team members by turning communication efforts into an internal PR campaign. Other leaders have certain negative assumptions (Adherence Enemy #3) about their teams and are uncomfortable letting go of their own interpretation of the values. They want to dictate the meaning of each value to every employee because, as the leader, they feel they know best. Be cautious if this is your tendency because **those who underestimate the intelligence of others tend to overestimate their own.** Think about it.

Instead, communicating values should be a natural outgrowth of your passion for the team's One Thing. It is best to simply describe some behaviors that demonstrate each value. This helps employees understand the intended spirit of the values and minimizes misinterpretations. For instance, a team value of "the customer is always right" can be interpreted many ways, so providing some examples would help define the acceptable boundaries and intent of that statement.

Ultimately, for values to come to life and become more than a plaque on the wall, team members must see them as personally meaningful. Your team's values can create an important, emotional connection for employees. The key to developing passion is to allow team members to interpret or internalize the values as their own by having them ask questions such as:

> What do these values mean to me?

> How do these values make me feel?

> Is my on-the-job behavior consistent with these values?

> How can I do my job differently to better reflect these values?

If *you* do not value your team's values, no one else will. Take the time to communicate your team's values, and more importantly, live them!

"Communicate, communicate, communicate – until you are sick of hearing yourself. Then communicate some more."
– Jack Welch, Former CEO of General Electric

Applying *Personal* Passion

Dr. Taryn Rose followed her passion. She was a successful medical resident in orthopedic surgery and had invested 13 years into her medical training. She also had a passion for fashion. So when it came to her shoes, like many women, she chose style over comfort. As a surgeon, she spent many long hours on her feet correcting other women's feet from the effects of damaging shoes.

With her own feet aching, she decided there had to be better options for stylish and comfortable shoes for herself and thousands of other women. As a result, Dr. Rose left her years of training, good salary and stable environment behind and started a women's shoe business. She now runs an $8 million high-end shoe company, and her shoes are worn by many physicians and celebrities.

Those who choose to create their own path and follow their passion are immensely rewarded on every level. In addition to experiencing a tremendous sense of purpose and contribution, many people who chart their own course reap significant financial rewards for following their passion, just like Taryn Rose.

Adherence Enemy #4 – Outside-in Approach

Many leaders take an outside-in approach with their teams – they attempt to change their teams before changing themselves. They want their teams to be more focused, but they do not model focused behavior themselves. Although an outside-in approach can produce short-term change, it will never produce long-term, sustainable change. In fact, many organizational change efforts fail within the first eighteen months for exactly this reason – leaders take an outside-in approach to change.

Adherence works inside-out. You must start with yourself and lead by example. Effective team performance begins with effective personal performance. Leaders who attempt to impose changes on their team without participating in those changes will not be successful in adhering to their plans.

High-achieving leaders start with themselves.

"If you want to be successful, put your effort into controlling the sail, not the wind."
– Anonymous

GETTING STARTED

You don't have to be great
to start, but you have
to start to be great.
– Zig Ziglar

Adherence At-A-Glance

Component	Success Factors
FOCUS	➤ Find your One Thing ➤ Know when to say "No" ➤ Keep it simple
COMPETENCE	➤ Elevate the average ➤ Get systematic ➤ Balance your view
PASSION	➤ Paint the picture ➤ Give what you want ➤ Value your values

Focus x **Competence** x **Passion** = **Adherence**

For high-achieving leaders, the pursuit of knowledge is important, but the pursuit of *self*-knowledge is critical to the effective execution of their plans. Knowing yourself and your team yields practical wisdom. Wisdom has little to do with age or experience, so do not get lulled into thinking you will become wise by virtue of time alone. Learn as much about yourself and your team as you possibly can.

As you continue your journey toward better Adherence, keep continuous learning a priority to develop your personal competence. Use life as your classroom. Search for best practices everywhere. Watch the people around you for examples of how to stick to it. You can learn from a great leader at your church, a speaker at a professional association meeting, or a particularly helpful salesperson at a local department store. Observe, read, ask, listen and learn.

Before you can start your journey toward Adherence, you have to know *where* you are starting from. As stated earlier, your greatest liability is the one you are *un*aware of. **Stop right now and take a moment to complete the quick assessment on the following page.** It will help you in two ways. First, it will identify your starting point by measuring your team's current level of Adherence. Second, it will help you discover opportunities to improve your team's Adherence.

Adherence Assessment

Circle your response to each statement. Refer to the Scoring section on the next page to calculate and interpret your score.

Adherence Component	Always	5	4	3	2	1	Never
1. Focus							
a. Our purpose is clear to all team members.		5	4	3	2	1	
b. It is easy to say "No" to initiatives that do not clearly fit my team's strategy.		5	4	3	2	1	
c. Plans for achieving my team's goals are kept very simple.		5	4	3	2	1	
Focus subtotal = _____							
2. Competence							
a. I establish SMART goals for myself and each team member.		5	4	3	2	1	
b. I have systems in place to ensure consistent and predictable performance by my team.		5	4	3	2	1	
c. I track key indicators of both past and projected team performance.		5	4	3	2	1	
Competence subtotal = _____							
3. Passion							
a. My team understands our plans, their roles and rewards.		5	4	3	2	1	
b. I demonstrate a genuine respect for each team member.		5	4	3	2	1	
c. I use our team values to help make day-to-day decisions.		5	4	3	2	1	
Passion subtotal = _____							
Focus x Competence x Passion = ADHERENCE							
_____ x _____ x _____ = _____							

Adherence Assessment Scoring

First, add the numbers you circled to calculate a subtotal for each component of Adherence. Next, input your subtotals in the formula at the bottom to determine your total Adherence score. You have to **multiply** your subtotals, so get out your calculator!

The wide range of possible scores on this assessment reflects the exponential effect of building Adherence (remember the bamboo seed). Higher scores for each component of Adherence have a multiplier effect on your total score.

Here is how to interpret your total Adherence score:

1,728 - 3,375 – You have high Adherence to your plans. Keep building on your momentum!

729 - 1,727 – Your Adherence could be better. To improve, develop your lagging components.

27 - 728 – Your scores on all three components were low – start by building a clear Focus for your team as a foundation for Adherence.

Sticking To It

Okay, now the ball is in your court. What are you going to do? **Take action:**

1. Review your Adherence component subtotal scores and identify the one where you have the biggest opportunity for improvement. Within that component, find the specific statement on the assessment that you rated lowest. **This is where you should start** to improve your Adherence.

   In addition to developing their weaknesses, high-achieving leaders leverage their strengths. Make sure you also identify your strongest Adherence component and then leverage it. Use that strength to help you build the other components that may need some work.

2. Go back and reread the chapter that corresponds to your weakest component, paying close attention to the success factor you rated lowest. Now, **commit to one action YOU can take in the next 24 hours** to start improving your Adherence. Start with an example you read or use a tip that seems particularly relevant to your team.

   High-achieving leaders start with themselves – they use an inside-out approach. They build personal Adherence before they try to build their team's Adherence. If the Assessment indicated your team's focus is low, examine your personal focus. If your team's competence is sub-par, check your own competence. If your team's passion is faltering, look at your personal passion.

   Whatever action you choose to take, it must start with you. Write your action as a present, personal and positive statement. Here are some examples:

   > I determine and communicate my team's One Thing.

   > I stop doing three things that do not support my One Thing.

> I establish SMART goals for myself.

> I identify and monitor leading indicators of my team's performance.

> I consistently communicate the big picture to my team.

> I live my team's values.

3. **Turn your action into a positive habit.** It takes 28 days of action and reinforcement to nurture a new, positive habit, so make your choice carefully. You want to become a high achiever, not an over-achiever, so stick to one action until you create a positive habit. It is better to make fewer commitments to yourself and keep them, than load up on commitments and watch yourself gradually falter (e.g., New Year's resolutions).

Share your commitment with others who want you to succeed. This will provide you with critical support for sticking to it and will keep you accountable to someone else.

After 28 days, come back to this book and commit to another action that will improve your Adherence. Build another positive habit from that action. Take baby steps, one at a time, to help keep your focus and to create successes upon which you can build confidence and momentum. **Achieving Adherence, like any other form of greatness, is not achieved overnight.**

Finally, mark your calendar for six months from now. Come back and retake the Adherence Assessment. If you have diligently followed the steps outlined above, you will see that your team's Adherence score has grown exponentially – just like that bamboo seed!

That's it. It is as simple as **1, 2, 3**. You are on your way to building Adherence.

Now, continue your journey by *STICKING TO IT!*

"Nothing in the world
can take the place of Persistence.
Talent will not;
nothing is more common
than unsuccessful men with talent.
Genius will not;
unrewarded genius is almost a proverb.
Education will not;
the world is full of educated derelicts.
Persistence and determination
alone are omnipotent."

– Calvin Coolidge

Five ways to reinforce
Sticking to It

1. **Keynote Presentation**
   Invite the authors to present a high-energy, engaging look at how today's top achievers stick to it...and how your team can do the same!

2. **Workshop**
   Delivered by one of the authors or a certified facilitator, this half- or full-day interactive workshop delivers simple tools that participants can put to work right away to boost their personal and team execution.

3. **Manager's PowerPoint® Briefing Presentation**
   Introduce and reinforce the adherence equation to your team with this professionally designed 48-slide presentation. Use the presentation for staff, brown bag lunches or as a follow-up development tool.

4. **Facilitator's PowerPoint® Presentation**
   This detailed and professionally designed, 118-slide presentation equips you to confidently and competently present all the key points and insights from *Sticking to It*. Perfect for training your entire organization.

5. **Learning Reinforcement Series**
   This powerful series of curated emails and video clips helps you reinforce the Adherence components of Focus, Competence and Passion so your team will stick to it!

THE L GROUP
Leadership at every level.

Consulting: Our top-notch consultants deliver cut-through-the-clutter insights that drive results for your team.

Executive Coaching: Our advisors help executives boost team and personal performance.

Speaking: Engage your team with passionate delivery and equip them with practical tools.

Resources: Rapid-read books, training tools, leadership assessments, note cards and posters to reinforce team values.

Training: Rely on our certified facilitators (English or Spanish speaking) or use our just-add-water training kits for internal delivery.

Other Books by the Authors:

107 Ways to Stick to It
A perfect companion to the best-selling book, *Sticking to It*. A practical and inspiring set of quick tips used by the most successful people. Guaranteed to help you achieve the success you deserve!

7 Moments…That Define Excellent Leaders
The difference between average and excellent can be found in moments … literally. These moments shape the leaders we are and the leaders we will become. Seize the moment to read and apply, and you will be one step closer to leadership excellence!

Leadership Matters: Daily Insights to Inspire Extraordinary Results.
The 31 matters of leadership will guide you through a daily journey to inspire extraordinary results. The topics are presented in a daily format designed for today's information-rich, time-poor world. Each mini-chapter ends with reflection questions to help you bridge the gap between insight and application.

Orchestrating Attitude: Getting the Best from Yourself and Others
Cut through the clutter to define simple actions for getting the best from yourself and others. Learn how your choice of thoughts, words and actions can create the kind of life you want.

Power Exchange: Boosting Accountability and Performance in Today's Workforce
Today's changing workforce requires powerful leadership. This quick read offers simple steps to help any leader boost accountability and performance in today's workforce.

Passionate Performance: Engaging Minds and Hearts to Conquer the Competition
This best-seller offers practical strategies to engage the minds and hearts of your team. Read it and conquer your competition!

The Nature of Excellence
Stunning photography and inspirational quotes are combined in this gift book. Through the twin lens of insight and imagery, you'll discover the natural excellence that surrounds us. You will also learn from the wisdom of more than 100 successful people who have inspired excellence throughout history.

Winners Always Quit: Seven Pretty Good Habits You Can Swap for Really Great Results
Successful people generally analyze, manage their time, get comfortable, strive for success, and show interest. They all sound pretty good, right? But what you are doing today may keep you from winning tomorrow. Learn how to quit today and you will never quit winning!

Order Form

1-30 copies $10.95	31-99 copies $9.95	100+ copies $7.95

Sticking to It: The Art of Adherence _____ copies X _____ = $ _____

Sticking to It Companion Resources

Manager's PowerPoint® Briefing Presentation	_____	X $99.95	= $ _____
Facilitator's Power Point® Presentation	_____	X $249.95	= $ _____

Other Books by the Authors

107 Ways to Stick to It	_____ copies X $10.95	= $ _____
7 Moments … That Define Excellent Leaders	_____ copies X $14.95	= $ _____
Leadership Matters	_____ copies X $16.95	= $ _____
Orchestrating Attitude	_____ copies X $10.95	= $ _____
Power Exchange	_____ copies X $10.95	= $ _____
Passionate Performance	_____ copies X $10.95	= $ _____
The Nature of Excellence	_____ copies X $15.95	= $ _____
Winners Always Quit	_____ copies X $14.95	= $ _____
The ULTIMATE ADVANTAGE Series	_____ packs X $27.95	= $ _____

(Includes *Sticking to It, Passionate Performance*
& *Orchestrating Attitude*)

Shipping & Handling $ _____

Subtotal $ _____

Sales Tax (8.25%-TX Only) $ _____

Total (U.S. Dollars Only) $ _____

Shipping and Handling Charges

Total $ Amount	Up to $49	$50-$99	$100-$249	$250-$1199	$1200-$3000	$3000+
Charge	$7	$9	$16	$30	$80	$125

Name _____ Job Title _____

Organization _____ Phone _____

Shipping Address _____ Fax _____

Billing Address _____ Email _____
(required when ordering PowerPoint Presentation)

City _____ State _____ Zip _____

❏ Please invoice (Orders over $200) Purchase Order Number (if applicable) _____

Charge Your Order: ❏ MasterCard   ❏ Visa   ❏ American Express

Credit Card Number _____ Exp. Date _____

Signature _____

❏ Check Enclosed (Payable to: CornerStone Leadership)

Mail

Phone 972.298.8377
Fax 972.274.2884   **www.CornerStoneLeadership.com**   **P.O. Box 764087**
Dallas, TX 75376

Thank you for reading *Sticking to It: The Art of Adherence*.
We hope it has assisted you in your quest for
personal and professional growth.

CornerStone Leadership is committed to provide new
and enlightening products to organizations worldwide.
Our mission is to fuel knowledge with practical resources
that will accelerate your team's productivity,
success and job satisfaction!

Best wishes for your continued success.

Leadership Institute

www.CornerStoneLeadership.com

Start a crusade in your organization –
have the courage to learn, the vision to lead,
and the passion to share.